Copyright © 2025 Scott Matthews

All rights reserved.

No part of this publication may be reproduced, stored in a retrieval system, or transmitted in any form or by any means—electronic, mechanical, photocopying, recording, or otherwise—without the prior written permission of the publisher, except for brief quotations used in reviews or scholarly works.

This book is intended for entertainment purposes only. While every effort has been made to ensure accuracy and appropriateness, the publisher and author make no guarantees and accept no responsibility for any misuse or misunderstanding of the content.

All jokes and illustrations are works of humor and wordplay. Any resemblance to actual persons, living or dead, is purely coincidental—or just a really funny accident.

Dedicated to the silent laughers—the ones who snort, wheeze, and cry silently with joy or pain. You're my people.

Welcome to the Pun-iverse!

You've just opened a book filled with puns so clever, so silly, and so eye-roll-inducing, you may need a helmet. This isn't just a collection of jokes—it's a comedy adventure in wordplay form. Whether you're a proud punster, a reluctant groaner, or someone who just appreciates a well-placed pun, you're in the right place.

Each page brings you a pun paired with a playful cartoon-style illustration, because let's face it—sometimes the visual pun-chline makes all the difference.

Read it front to back, flip randomly, or force your friends and family to listen to "just one more." We won't judge. (Well, maybe your friends will.)

Now turn the page… and let the puns begin!

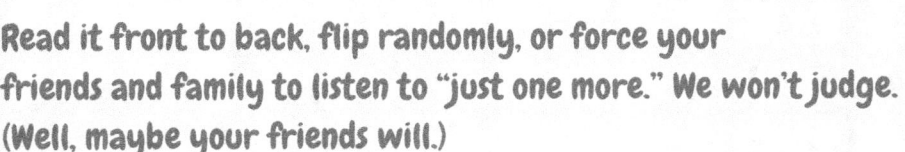

I got hired at the zoo.
The pay is bananas.

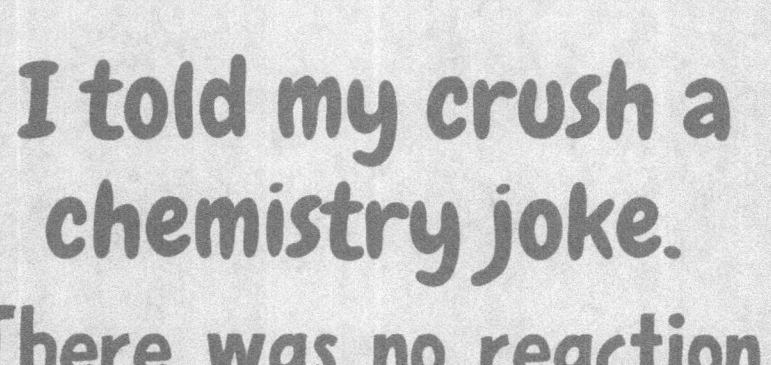

What do you call a parade of rabbits hopping backward? A receding hare-line.

I was going to make a joke about an elevator, but it's an uplifting experience.

What do you call a fake noodle? An impasta!

Why did the coffee file a police report? It got mugged.

What do you call cheese that isn't yours?

Nacho cheese.

What do you call a sleeping bull?
A bulldozer.

What do you call a bear with no teeth?
A gummy bear.

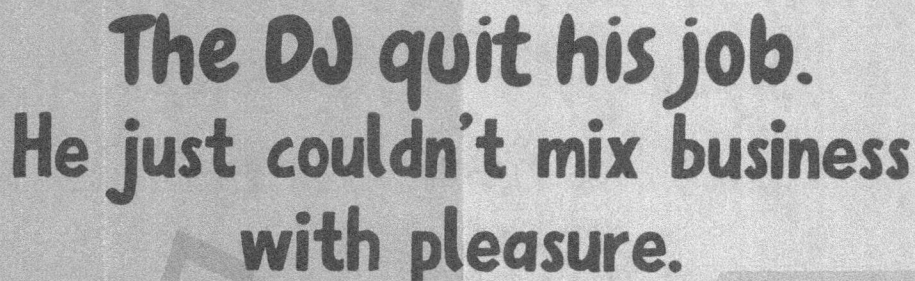

I'm writing a book about reverse psychology. Please don't read it.

What do you call a factory that makes good products?
A satis-factory.

I'm trying to organize a hide and seek contest, but good players are hard to find.

I used to work at a blanket factory,

but it folded.

What do you get when you cross a snowman and a vampire?
Frostbite.

I walked into a lamppost yesterday.

It was enlightening.

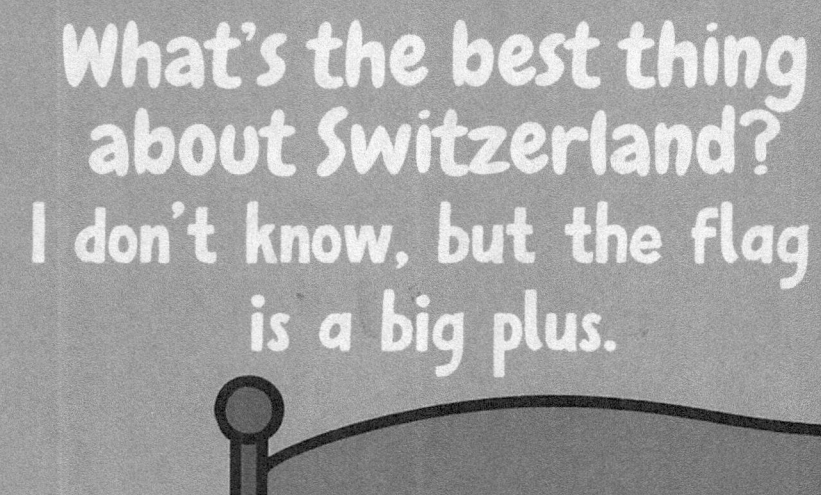

Why don't eggs tell jokes?
They'd crack each other up.

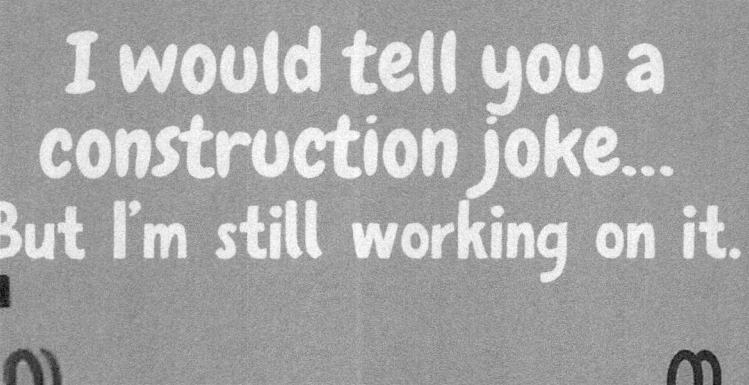

I opened a bakery in space.
It's called
"Planet of the Crepes."

I considered becoming a chef,

I couldn't meat the expectations.

I asked the librarian if the library had any books on paranoia.

She whispered, "They're right behind you."

I used to hate facial hair...
but then it grew on me.

The shovel was a groundbreaking invention.

What did the duck say when it bought lipstick?

"Put it on my bill."

Geometry is just plane fun.

I gave all my batteries away.
They were free of charge.

www.ingramcontent.com/pod-product-compliance
Lightning Source LLC
Chambersburg PA
CBHW052211090526
44584CB00019BA/3047